The sea and surf in Canada's Ocean Playground - photo courtesy C.N.R.

Picture Perfect Nova Scotia
A Guide to Canada's Ocean Playground

TEXT BY PAUL McCORMICK

Edited by Gladys Burchell - Layout & Design by Charles Burchell & Creative Edge Graphics

CONTENTS

Anyone in a hurry may take the new controlled-access highways,
from which they may debouch whenever and wherever they wish.

 # ISTORY

EXTERIOR VIEW OF PORT ROYAL HABITATION *Near today's town of Annapolis Royal, this replica of the original Habitation, built by Champlain in 1605, may be visited. It occupies the exact site of the first building and is exact in size and detail. Throughout the building all timber framing has been mortised, tenoned and pinned together in the old manner, no spikes or nails being used. It was here at the Habitation that Champlain founded "THE ORDER OF GOOD CHEER".*

Civilization in Nova Scotia dates back at least 10,000 years. Near Debert, in Colchester County, archaeologists have found tools and artifacts made by paleo-Indians, along with other evidence of a twenty acre Stone Age village.

When Europeans arrived in Nova Scotia some 500 years ago, there was already a thriving Micmac Indian culture. At first, white civilization had little impact. John Cabot and his son Sebastian landed near Bay St. Lawrence, Cape Breton in 1497. By 1521 there were Portuguese Fishermen using the Ingonish area as a summer fishing base. In Canso Harbour, during the same period, the French had established a similar base on Grassy Island. But with the founding of European settlements in the next century, the native way of life went into decline.

It is probably fair to say that the history of Nova Scotia has been a miniature version of world events at large. The major wars of the last four centuries have often been played out in reduced scale. Treaties signed thousands of miles away have affected the territory, population and government of this province.

In 1604 Henry VI of France granted Sieur de Monts a fur-trading monopoly for the new world. Accompanying him as geographer was Samuel de Champlain, as well as two shiploads of prospective colonists. They spent a disastrous first winter on an island in the mouth of the St. Croix River, which now marks the boundary between Maine and New Brunswick. What remained of the colony was moved across the Bay of Fundy the following spring to the shores of the Annapolis Basin. Here they built a palisaded town from local timber. Near this "Habitation" they planted gardens and dammed a stream as a trout pond. Having assured their survival, Champlain created the Order of Good Cheer to entertain the colony throughout the long winter. Each member would serve, in turn, as Chief Steward for the evening meal. The meals and accompanying ceremonies grew more complex as each tried to outdo the previous steward. The local Indians were invited to attend, with twenty to thirty sharing the free bread nightly. Even the great Membertou and his fellow chiefs became members of the continent's first social club. For two years Port Royal thrived and then de Monts' monopoly was cancelled.

In an attempt to save the colony, de Monts appointed an officer, by the name of Poutrincourt, Lieutenant Governor of Port Royal. Poutrincourt was able to persuade the king to uphold his appointment, and although Port Royal itself was destroyed by the English in 1613, it is from these original colonists that many of the province's Acadians today trace their ancestry.

CHAMPLAIN'S "ORDER OF GOOD CHEER", FROM A RARE PAINTING BY C.W. JEFFERYS *This ceremony was initiated by Samuel de Champlain shortly after founding the "Habitation" at Port Royal in 1604. The Order of Good Times, as it was also called, helped to pass the long winter nights. Each night one of the French Colonists provided the meal for the settlement, and there was much competition as to who was the most successful host. The meal was served with much pomp and ceremony as this picture depicts. Photo courtesy of the Public Archives of Canada.*

While France was busy settling the St. Lawrence River Valley, England had successfully established colonies to the south. It was natural that they would also wish to lay claim to the whole eastern seaboard of North America.

Nova Scotia is Latin for "New Scotland". In 1621, Sir William Alexander, a Scottish nobleman, was granted the land which today forms Nova Scotia and New Brunswick. His scheme was to sell it off in grants to English gentlemen who wished to become baronets. The titles, rather than the land, seemed of utmost interest to the buyers, and most never set foot in the new world. A coat of arms bearing the Scottish flag, a flag still flown with pride by Nova Scotians, was also granted to the province.

In 1632 Nova Scotia was officially ceded back to France. For the remainder of the century, Acadia prospered, and French settlements sprung up throughout the Annapolis Valley and Chignecto Isthmus; the settlers reclaimed low-lying marshes for pasture land through the construction of dykes. In 1713, the territory again returned to England, with the exception of what is today Prince Edward Island and Cape Breton.

The French soon made the most of Cape Breton's strategic location at the mouth of the Gulf of St. Lawrence. Over a period of 24 years, they constructed a massive stone fortress on the harbour at Louisbourg. In addition to the fortress, harbour batteries and lighthouse, a town covering 50 acres sheltered by a two-mile-long earthenworks and masonry wall was built to provide the commercial,

FORT ANNE NATIONAL HISTORIC PARK *The present Fort Anne is the fourth fort to occupy this 28 acre site in beautiful Annapolis Royal, the first having been built in 1635. The town of Annapolis Royal was founded in 1605 and is the oldest non-native settlement in Canada.*

military and government centre for the colony.

Although massive in size, its actual fortifications were weak, and in 1745 a band of New England volunteers successfully captured Louisbourg. This feat did not rate highly on the scale of world events and in 1748 the British handed the fortress back to France.

England's answer to the renewed threat of Louisbourg was to establish its own fortress in Nova Scotia. In 1749, Halifax was founded and construction of the first Citadel began.

In 1758 the British, this time under the command of General James Wolfe, once again captured Louisbourg. Two years later, British Prime Minister William Pitt ordered its total destruction.

Meanwhile, from his new capital in Halifax, Governor Cornwallis was consolidating Britain's hold on Nova Scotia. In the fall of 1755, the order went out for the deportation of the Acadians.

The reasons behind Expulsion of the Acadians are to this day hotly debated. The "official" reason given for the order was the refusal by these farmers to sign a written oath of loyalty to the British Crown. Often overlooked is the argument that for half a century of British rule the Acadians had coexisted peacefully with their English neighbours, and had never resisted swearing an oral oath of allegiance. If the deportation was only in answer to a question of security, then why were families split up and sent on different ships to different locations in New England? Many Acadians made their way from the Thirteen Colonies south to Louisiana, where their descendants, the "Cajuns", live to this day. Others took to the woods avoiding

HISTORIC LOUISBOURG *Here stood the Fortress, a town covering more than 50 acres, the French stronghold in the New World. More than 20 years in the building (1720-44), its fortifications were hardly finished when war broke out between England and France. Louisbourg was founded, captured in 1745, handed back to the French in 1748, recaptured by Wolfe in 1758, and ordered demolished, all in less than 50 years. This reconstruction is the largest undertaking in Canada and is done in exact detail, with furnishings of the period.*

expulsion, eventually making their way to isolated areas of Nova Scotia, New Brunswick or even Quebec, establishing communities which still retain the Acadian culture. Even more made their way back from expulsion after the initial furore had died out. Henry Wadsworth Longfellow's poem "Evangeline" chronicles one such pair of star-crossed Acadian lovers.

The government wasted no time in opening the rich Acadian farmlands for settlement. The first group arrived between the Expulsion and the American War of Independence. These New England Planters were granted townships on former Acadian lands. They were joined by other "Pre-Loyalist" fishermen who settled along the South Shore of the province.

Lunenburg was settled by German, Swiss and Montbeliardian protestants in 1753, and on the other side of the province, Scottish immigration began with the landing of the Hector in Pictou in 1773. Over the next century, northern Nova Scotia and Cape Breton would see a flood of Scottish settlement.

The aftermath of the American War of Independence included a flood of Loyalist settlers to Nova Scotia. Shelburne and Liverpool were both settled by American colonists wishing to remain loyal to Britain.

Included in their number were former slaves who settled, for the most part, in Shelburne County and Preston, east of Halifax.

The War of Independence also brought boom times to the province's economy. Already healthy coastal towns found them-

EVANGELINE AND THE DEPARTURE OF GABRIEL, GRAND PRE
Evangeline watches the ship carrying Gabriel, her loved one, depart into the sunset. Evangeline is the tale of Acadia, written by Henry W. Longfellow, and this rare picture, dated 1885, forms the basis of his epic tale. This tale of the Acadian lovers of Grande Pre has enshrined in hearts of the world the tragic memory of the expulsion of two centuries ago.

selves growing wealthy from the spoils of "privateering", government-sanctioned piracy aimed at American shipping. It was a boost to a shipping industry that grew up naturally in the province, aided by timber for ship-building and Nova Scotia's situation on shipping lanes between Europe, New England and the Caribbean.

The potato famines in Ireland brought shiploads of Irish immigrants in the following century. The late-nineteenth and twentieth centuries have seen waves of immigrants seeking refuge from persecution, wars and destitution, with Eastern European Jews, Indo-Asians, Lebanese and orientals adding to the province's growing multicultural mix.

Nova Scotia was one of the four original partners in Canada's Confederation in 1867. Its men and women served in both world wars and continue to contribute to the advancement of research, knowledge and the global economy.

Wherever you travel in Nova Scotia you will find evidence of its rich history, with many historic sites, restorations and museums to delight the visitor and native, alike.

COURTYARD AT PORT ROYAL HABITATION—THE FIRST PERMANENT WHITE SETTLEMENT IN CANADA, 1605 *This is a replica of the original Port Royal Habitation which was built by Champlain in 1605. It is exact in size and detail, and built on the original site. As in the original building, no spikes or nails were used. The well shelter, seen here, is covered with oak shingles of the size used 300 years ago. It was here at this habitation, that Champlain founded "THE ORDER OF GOOD CHEER".*

THE LIGHTHOUSE ROUTE

THE SOUTH SHORE AND PEGGY'S COVE

YARMOUTH LIGHT *Shining brightly from atop its rocky perch, this lighthouse guides ships to safety in its fine harbour. Yarmouth, founded in 1761, is a popular tourist resort being serviced by two large motor vessels.*

Situated at the mouth of a long harbour running north from Cape Forchu on the western rim and Chebogue Point on the east, Yarmouth is the Canadian terminal for car ferries from Portland and Bar Harbour, Maine.

Yarmouth was settled during a wave of immigration from New England that saw 16 townships established along the province's South Shore during the 1750's and 60's.

South of Yarmouth there are the interspersed English and French communities of Argyle. Houses crowd together in narrow fishlots along the shoreline of settlements which are tucked behind islands and separated by deserted stretches of marsh and scrubland.

Continuing along the shoreline you come to the "Pubinicos". South of the Pubnico Harbour, villages take on a character familiar to visitors from the northeastern United States. Houses, many more than two centuries old, are simple Cape Cod saltboxes.

By far, the largest industry along the South Shore is the winter lobster fishery which lasts from the end of October until May.

This, along with the regular fishery, provides the basis for most other commercial and service-related businesses.

Where Route 103 passes through the township of Barrington, you will find the Barrington Woolen Mill Museum and, above the west bank of the river, the Old Meeting House. Built in 1765, it is the oldest non-conformist church in Canada, and one of a handful remaining in eastern North America. Ten minutes south of here is Cape Sable Island. At "The Hawk" on its seaward tip, you are as far south as you can be on either of Canada's coasts, which is the same latitude as Marseille, France. Along the south coast of Cape Sable is found a deserted white sand beach stretching for more than five miles. Across the bay near Sand Hills Beach, is a cairn marking the site of Fort St. Louis, constructed by Charles de la Tour in 1627 to guard his lucrative fur-trading interests around the Bay of Fundy.

Shelburne, the next town along the coast, was settled by Loyalists fleeing New England following the American Revolution. A stroll along the waterfront will take you past many of the original commercial buildings and houses. Ross Thompson House Museum is a period home and store stocked with furniture and merchandise from Shelburne's earliest years.

Continuing east across the Jordan River, the coastline juts outward towards Lockeport. Across the harbour is Louis Head Beach. Nearby Port L'Hebert marks the start of a sparsely settled conservation area of granite ledge, scrub, marsh and beach meadows which provide a haven for migrating wildfowl in the early fall of each year.

BLUE ROCKS *Scenic Blue Rocks is a favourite tourist spot, just five miles from Lunenburg on Nova Scotia's south shore. Its name is derived from the blue-gray rock ledges upon which the village stands.*

Many of the dirt roads along here that head towards the coast, lead to isolated stretches of virgin white sand beach. One community, Port Mouton (pronounced "matoon") was so named when a sheep from de Monts' 1604 mapping expedition fell overboard and was drowned.

The town of Liverpool, at the mouth of the Mersey River, was settled by New Englanders in 1759. These sailors and shipbuilders created a pretty little town along the banks of a river which flowed from virgin pine forest. The paper industry that grew up here was as natural a development as the "privateering" of the sailors in this settlement during the American Revolution. The rewards of this legal piracy can be seen in many of the stately homes. The home of Simeon Perkins, one of the early settlers, is a museum open to the public. There you can browse through his 1766 - 1812 diary and get a picture of colonial days along the South Shore.

Take Route 8 northward along the banks of the Mersey River through Caledonia to Kejimkujik National Park. The youngest of two national parks in Nova Scotia, "Kedgie" has been established to preserve and make accessible the natural features of the interior of the province. Its rivers and lakes were enjoyed by our natives for millennium before the Europeans came to the new world. Today it features modern camping, swimming and canoeing facilities and a year-round staff of guides, rangers and naturalists. Another forty-five minutes north of Kedgie is Annapolis Royal. It's not hard to see how Nova Scotians can boast that you are never more than an hour from the ocean. If you backtrack from Kejimkujik to South Brookfield and take

LIGHTHOUSE AND CANNON GUARDING LIVERPOOL HARBOUR *Liverpool is steeped in history from its early beginning in 1760 through the years of privateering to recent restoration of its historic houses. During the turbulent era of 1800, many residents shared in the outfitting of ships to sail on the high seas as "privateers", to defend their trade with the West Indies, and rage war upon the enemies of Great Britain. The "Rover" and the "Liverpool Packet" are two famous privateering ships. Visitors to Liverpool will also enjoy a visit to historic "Perkins House" filled with relics of the period. Books about the area are "THE ROVER, HIS MAJESTY'S YANKEES", and "PRIDE'S FANCY" by Thomas H. Raddall.*

Grand Pré

GLOOSCAP TRAIL

The trail is named after the legendary warrior who ruled the Micmacs. It follows the shores of Fundy, starting at the New Brunswick border and ending at Cape Blomidon. It is said that Glooscap lives on the cape watching over his children and animal friends from the bluff. He created islands when he slung mud at insolent beavers, and he scattered gems all over the beach when he tossed his grandmother's jewelry in the air. He also is responsible for creating the tides.

It is indeed an enchanted and mystical place. Tidal bores force rivers to flow backward. The tides recede so far it is possible to walk in fossilized dinosaur footprints on the bottom of the ocean.

The trail along the coast offers magnificent panaromic views from the bluffs. The road also winds through pastoral valleys, passing waterfalls, maple groves, and blueberry fields.

It is thought that Micmac Indians living near Mapleton discovered maple syrup when they boiled their potatoes in maple sap, inadvertently producing a sweet and thick substance. Today thousands of pounds of maple-sugar products are made here annually from the local groves on the Cobequid Mountains.

The world's highest tides have been recorded at Burncoat Head, the greatest difference between high and low tide measuring 54 feet. In spring and fall this is a popular feeding ground for thousands of migrating shorebirds.

Parrsboro holds a Rockhound Roundup each year for the many hobbyists who come to the Minas Basin looking for semi-precious stones. At low tide fishing boats and lumber freighters sit on dry land as if stranded in the middle of nowhere.

In 1985, near Parrsboro, geologists found the largest cache of fossilized bones ever discovered in North America, including very rare skulls and reptile jaws. Along Chignecto Bay, 40 foot tides have eroded the limestone of 100 foot high cliffs, revealing fish, amphibians, insects and trees fossilized while still standing.

The town of Springhill, once a coal mining centre, has been ravaged by several fires and mine-related tragedies. The Springhill Miner's Museum has underground tours and exhibits depicting the lives of those who worked and died underground. The Anne Murray Centre chronicles the life and career of the internationally famous recording star who was born and raised in this town.

Route 208, you have the option of visiting New Germany and following the LaHave River downstream to Bridgewater or travelling across the province via Route 10 to Middleton in the Annapolis Valley.

Along the coast between Bridgewater and Liverpool are many fine white sandy beaches in places such as Beach Meadows, Rissers Beach and Green Bay. A car ferry runs from West LaHave to Middle LaHave, while the road parallels the picturesque LaHave River to Bridgewater.

In Bridgewater there is the DesBrisay Museum National Exhibition Centre featuring exhibits interpreting the natural history, early settlement, culture and industry of Lunenburg County. From Bridgewater, you can cross the LaHave River and follow along as it makes its way to the Atlantic. The small town of Riverport features several large homes of the last century bearing testament to the prosperous fishing and trading ships which have sailed from this sheltered port. Nearby there are excellent white sandy beaches.

Lunenburg, as its name would suggest, was founded by German, Swiss and Montbeliardian Protestants in 1753. As one of the South Shore's most picturesque towns, the elegant sea-captains' houses and 18th and 19th century commercial buildings climb the steep harbour-side hill. Dominating the summit is Lunenburg Academy, with its Victorian roofline, colour scheme and trim.

Along the waterfront the huge wooden warehouses and shipyard workshops bear testament to this town's seafaring past. You can see the yards that produced the original Bluenose fishing

LUNENBURG, A PICTURESQUE SEA PORT ON NOVA SCOTIA'S SOUTH SHORE *This spectacular aerial view of Lunenburg town shows the excellent harbour, waterfront, town and some of the historic buildings. Bluenose I and II were both built here, and Bluenose I was the undefeated champion of the North Atlantic Fishing Fleet. This harbour has seen in later times rum - running ships, pirates, and privateers, and tales abound of these times. Photo courtesy Nova Scotia Museum.*

schooner, as well as the Bounty reproduction and the Bluenose II. Visit the Fisheries' Museum of the Atlantic for a comparison of the fisheries in the days of wooden saltbankers with modern steel-hulled trawlers.

From Lunenburg it is a twenty minute drive to Mahone Bay. This sheltered bay was also home to privateers. The American privateer, Young Teazer, was blown up in the bay by a British deserter on June 17, 1813. Locals claim you may see the ghostly Teazer burning on the horizon if you look seaward on the anniversary of this midsummer night.

The most notorious landmark in Mahone Bay is Oak Island. In 1796 three lads from Mahone Bay uncovered the mouth of a tunnel in a clearing among the oaks. At ten, twenty and thirty feet they found log platforms. Their discovery was to launch a futile two-century hunt for Captain Kidd's treasure that would eventually sink many shafts, cost many men's fortunes and six lives. One attempt was made by American Captain Henry L. Bowdoin in 1909. Bowdoin was the first to use "modern" drilling and mining techniques. Not many investors were attracted to his scheme, but one very famous backer had been fascinated with buried treasure since boyhood. He was Franklin D. Roosevelt. To date, this has been the "world's costliest treasure hunt."

Further along the bay at Chester Basin, Route 12 ventures across the interior of the province to Kentville. A short drive inland there are New Ross and the Ross Farm Museum, a functioning 19th century farm.

OAK ISLAND - THE WORLD'S COSTLIEST TREASURE HUNT *It is believed that the notorious pirate Captain Kidd buried a vast treasure on this island, and since 1795 countless adventurers and many well financed companies have sought to wrestle this great treasure from the "Money Pit", as it came to be called. Early attempts reached a depth of 96 feet when suddenly water rushed in flooding the "Pit". Many have died in the attempt. All have agreed that the designer of the "Pit" was a genius, for despite all attempts with today's sophisticated equipment, the treasure still remains hidden. More money has been spent here than on any other treasure hunt in the world.*

Again on the Atlantic coast there is the town of Chester, again dating from the 1760's. From here a passenger ferry runs to Big Tancook, one of 365 islands in Mahone Bay.

A drive around the Aspotogan Peninsula will reveal several beaches including Bayswater and Fox Point. The scenery here is very picturesque. It was here at Deep Cove that the millionaire industrialist, the late Cyrus Eaton, kept a summer home. Hubbards is situated at the western head of St. Margarets Bay and was founded about 1800. The white sands of Queensland and Black Point, nearby, will tempt many weary travellers to stop and cool their toes in the Atlantic surf.

Route 333 ventures seaward from Head of St. Margarets Bay through coastal communities to Peggy's Cove.

Whether the cove gets its name from the romantic tale of the lone survivor of a shipwreck who married a local fisherman or is merely the diminutive of the bay on which it is situated can be left to the visitor to decide.

The village perches on a huge 415 million year old Devonian granite ledge jutting into the North Atlantic. Huge boulders picked up and deposited by retreating glaciers more than 10,000 years ago seem randomly scattered in and around the village, creating an eerie setting. What little scrubby vegetation there is clings to the granular "Gibraltar soil".

Many of its population of some sixty souls can trace their ancestry back to the original six German families (three with

PRIZE YOKE OF OXEN AT ROSS FARM, NEW ROSS *Tourists will enjoy a visit to this farm, restored to its early 19th century appearance. It was started by Captain William Ross in August 1816, when he, his wife and children, along with 172 disbanded soldiers, settled here. Now complete with farm animals and relics, it depicts rural life as experienced by these early settlers. The farm is located between Chester Basin and Kentville. Photo courtesy Nova Scotia Museum.*

the name "Isenhauer") who settled here in 1811.

Peggy's is renowned with artists and photographers for its picturesque fishermen's shanties, surf crashing on granite ledges and the Peggy's Cove Lighthouse. Although it no longer functions as an operational navigation aid, the lighthouse does house a post office from which you can post cards and letters. Exercise extreme caution if you venture out onto the rocky ledges. The high surf, slippery footing, and fierce undertow have washed many to a watery grave.

FUN IN THE SUN - NOVA SCOTIA'S SOUTH SHORE *One of the many advantages to living near the sea is the abundance of beautiful sand beaches. Pictured here is Queensland Beach, just a short drive from Halifax on the Lighthouse Route.*

AERIAL VIEW, LIGHTHOUSE, PEGGY'S COVE *The result of the melting ice age has left Peggy's Cove area "barren rock", as seen here. Thousands of tourists come every year to view this "rugged beauty", climb the rocks, and see the pounding surf. During storms the spray from the heavy sea often surges atop the lighthouse.*

PEGGY'S POINT LIGHTHOUSE *The original lighthouse was built in 1868. This modern lighthouse is a popular tourist spot located on the south side of Peggy's Cove. The large rocks (estimated up to 90 tons) have been washed up in storms of past years.*

PEGGY'S COVE *The fishing village of Peggy's cove has been preserved by the Government so that this desolate yet awe inspiring scene will remain unchanged. In this view the fishermen, their sheds and many lobster pots on the wharf offer a typical rustic panorama.*

A TRIBUTE TO THE FISHERMEN OF PEGGY'S COVE *Completed by Canadian marine artist William de Garthe shortly before his death, this monument serves as a tribute to the fishermen's way of life. Two of de Garthe's murals can be seen inside St. John's Anglican Church in Peggy's Cove.*

TWILIGHT - PEGGY'S COVE *A time of beauty is enjoyed as these boats rest peacefully beside the small wooden wharves. Peggy's Cove, with its lighthouse, fish sheds and cottages perched about them, has been a paradise for artists for many years.*

AERIAL VIEW OF PEGGY'S COVE *Every season finds tourists, artists, and photographers visiting both the cove and lighthouse. The cove was named after an early settler, and first appeared on a map made in 1811. The surf on Lighthouse Point is spectacular, especially after an easterly storm, but can be dangerous. The rustic appeal found here is enjoyed by all in Canada's Ocean Playground.*

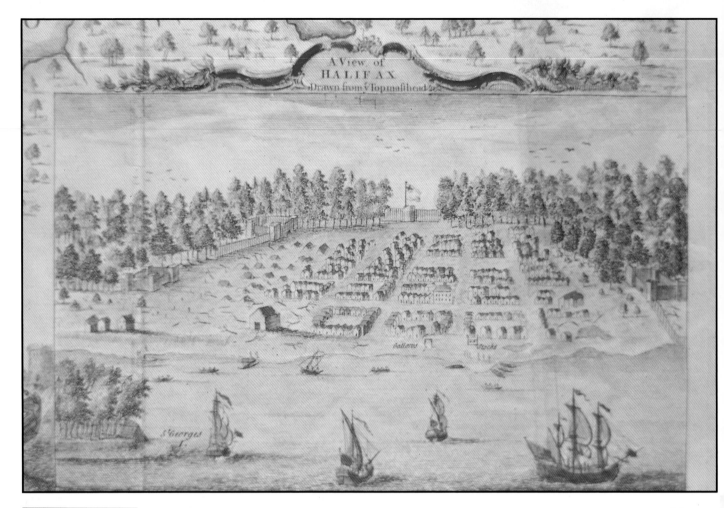

A VIEW OF HALIFAX *Halifax was founded in 1749. This view circa 1750 shows the first "Citadel" and Harbour. Photo courtesy Parks Canada.*

HALIFAX AND DARTMOUTH

THE TWIN CITIES

The City of Halifax was founded on a tree-covered granite peninsula by Colonel Edward Cornwallis on June 21, 1749. Peninsular Halifax is foot-shaped with a ten-mile long, deep natural harbour opening into a large sheltered basin which forms the heel, and the Northwest Arm which defines the toe.

Halifax harbour is the largest ice-free port on the east coast of North America and the world's second largest natural harbour. The Port of Halifax has two container terminals and modern grain and cargo handling facilities.

The first European settlers were the English. They were followed by the French, Scottish, Irish, Germans and Blacks from the United States and Caribbean.

The strategic location of Halifax Harbour makes it the ideal headquarters for Maritime Command, one of three operational commands of the Canadian Armed Forces. A fleet of some 20 warships are permanently stationed here. Canadian Forces Base Halifax is the largest in the country.

Historically a centre of trade and commerce, the Halifax-Dartmouth Metro Area is the largest retail area and distribution centre in Atlantic Canada.

Halifax is the capital of Nova Scotia. As well as the seat of provincial government, the Metro Area is home to nine hospitals and seven degree-granting universities and colleges.

The best way to see Halifax is by water. Narrated tours leave Historic Properties in the downtown core several times daily. The twin cities of Halifax and Dartmouth are linked by two of the world's longest suspension bridges, the A. Murray MacKay and Angus L. Macdonald.

Citadel Hill, in the centre of downtown Halifax offers a vantage point from which you can view the length of the harbour from McNab's and George's Islands at the mouth, through the Narrows with its bridges, to Bedford Basin. Citadel Hill National Historic Park is Canada's most visited historic site. The present fortifications are the fourth built on the site and are little changed since the British abandonment in 1906.

The first wooden stockade was built with the founding of Halifax in 1749. It was followed by five small forts within a wooden palisade constructed as protection from the Americans in 1776. The Napoleonic Wars spurred construction of the third fort by Queen Victoria's father, Prince Edward, in 1793. By the turn of that century, the wood and earthworks fortifications were already crumbling.

To be fair to Edward, it should be noted that other

AERIAL VIEW OF THE STAR SHAPED CITADEL HILL, HARBOUR AND BRIDGES *This "world famous" fort was started in 1749, the year Edward Cornwallis founded Halifax. Visitors come from all over the world to see this historic site, visit its three fine museums and have their picture taken by the Old Town Clock. The 12:00 o'clock cannon is still fired daily from here, marking the noon hour. A panoramic view of the harbour and city can be viewed from here. Photo courtesy Parks Canada.*

OLD TOWN CLOCK, HALIFAX *Erected in 1803, the Old Town Clock is one of Halifax's oldest and most famous landmarks. Located on the harbour side of Citadel Hill, it stands as a reminder of our heritage amid the modern architecture of a growing city.*

HALIFAX PUBLIC GARDENS *Established in 1867, these gardens were based on the gardens of 1753. This bandstand was erected in 1887 to celebrate the Golden Jubilee of Queen Victoria. Summer concerts are still enjoyed amid the colourful and fragrant landscape.*

fortifications undertaken by him, such as the Martello Tower at Point Pleasant Park, have stood the test of time. And this is a fitting tribute to a man who valued time. To ensure the punctuality of those under his command, Prince Edward ordered the construction of the Town Clock in 1803 which still graces the hill.

It took two attempts, lasting from 1829 to 1848, to complete the present fort. The noon gun has been fired from Citadel Hill daily since 1800. The guns have never been fired in anger.

If you look to the west of the Citadel, your view is of the Wanderers' Grounds and the Commons. Part of the defense system, this slope was left free from development as the city grew. Today it is the heart of Halifax's recreational programs.

On the southern edge of the commons is the Nova Scotia Museum, headquarters of a network of provincial museums. A block away is the 17 acre Public Gardens. From a five-acre garden in 1753, North America's only public Victorian garden has grown to feature an outstanding collection of Victorian carpet flower beds, weeping trees, formal plantings, a concert bandstand and duck pond.

Many fine examples of colonial and Victorian architecture exist on the slopes between Citadel Hill and the harbour. Historic Properties, on the harbour front, is a collection of stores, warehouses and businesses dating from the early 1800s which today house shops, restaurants and offices. Privateers Wharf is the permanent home of Bluenose II. The upper floors of much of Historic Properties form the campus of the Nova Scotia College of Art and Design.

ST. PAUL'S CHURCH *Located opposite City Hall on the south end of Halifax's Parade Ground stands Canada's oldest Protestant Church, St. Paul's. It was officially opened on September 2, 1750 with Rev. William Tutty officiating. The original building was an exact replica of St. Peter's Church in London. One of the most fascinating aspects of St. Paul's is the silhouette of one of the early clergymen imprinted in a window on the western side of the church by the Halifax Explosion in 1917.*

Walk along the harbour front past the law courts, ferry terminal and Cable Wharf to the Maritime Museum of the Atlantic. Tied up at the pier is the early twentieth century hydrographic ship Acadia, open to the public. Visit the museum for a picture of life on the Atlantic coast.

Continue along the harbour or cross Lower Water Street and walk uphill past the Old Post Office, constructed between 1863 and 1868 as a new provincial building. At the corner of George and Hollis Streets sits Province House, constructed in 1819. A statue on the grounds of Canada's first legislative building commemorates Joseph Howe, who won freedom of the press for the North American Colonies.

At the corner of Barrington and Duke Streets is Halifax City Hall. Built in 1890, City Hall fronts the Grand Parade, an old militia drilling ground. St. Paul's Church is at the other end of the Grand Parade. Built in 1749, the first year of settlement, St. Paul's is the first English protestant church to have been built in Canada.

At the southern tip of peninsular Halifax is a forested parkland with sandy beach known as Point Pleasant Park. Once a military preserve guarding the harbour mouth — as the remnants of batteries and Martello Tower evidence — in 1866 the Crown granted a 999 year lease to the Park Commission for an annual rent of one shilling.

St. Mary's University, to the north of Point Pleasant, was established in 1802 and is the oldest English-speaking Roman Catholic

HISTORIC PROPERTIES, HALIFAX WATERFRONT *Today Historic Properties is an unique blend of old world shops, boutiques, and restaurants. In days past, however, some of these same buildings were used to store the booty of the privateers who sailed around the world from Halifax.*

ALMOST ONE MILE LONG, THE ANGUS L. MACDONALD BRIDGE SPANS HALIFAX HARBOUR *This bridge is the second longest suspension bridge in the British Commonwealth, 5,239 feet in length. It is one of the two bridges which link Halifax and Dartmouth and was opened in 1955. Halifax was founded in 1749 by Edward Cornwallis, and has one of the finest harbours in the world.*

FERRY TERMINAL, DARTMOUTH *The Halifax-Dartmouth ferry service is the oldest operating salt-water service in Canada. The original ferry was operated by John Connor who received a charter from Governor Edward Cornwallis in 1752, just three years after the founding of Halifax.*

University in Canada. It is second only in size to Dalhousie, which is located to the west, on University Avenue. In between can be found several teaching hospitals and medical faculties.

In Halifax's North End, between the two harbour bridges and bounded by Barrington and Robie Streets, is the area most damaged in the December 6, 1917 Halifax Explosion. When the explosives-laden French ship, Mont Blanc, collided with the Belgian Relief ship, Imo, it sent a column of fire two miles high and levelled two square miles of the city. It was the largest man-made explosion ever unleashed before the atomic bomb. One thousand six hundred and fifty people died immediately and thousands were left injured and homeless. Today, on the site of Fort Needham, at Novalea and Devonshire Streets, the Halifax Explosion Memorial Bell Tower sits overlooking the harbour as a permanent memorial.

Leave Halifax on Route 2 and drive along the Bedford Basin for a panoramic view of the harbour, bridges and twin cities.

HALIFAX - SPECTACULAR NIGHT-TIME COLOUR *The Halifax skyline at night promises the excitement that only Atlantic Canada's largest city can offer. Whether your pleasure is history, nightlife, shopping or quiet relaxation, Halifax has it all and much more.*

THE EVANGELINE TRAIL

WESTERN NOVA SCOTIA AND THE FUNDY SHORE

APPLE BLOSSOMS AT CAPE BLOMIDON *Discover the beauty of Nova Scotia's Annapolis Valley. From apple orchards and rich, rolling farm land to the world's highest tides in the Bay of Fundy, the Annapolis Valley has something to offer any visitor.*

At the tip of the peninsula forming the western mouth of Yarmouth Harbour is Cape Forchu and the Yarmouth Light, signalling the entrance to the Bay of Fundy. From Yarmouth, Route 1 follows the coastline of the Bay of Fundy through Clare District along St. Mary's Bay, past Digby into the Annapolis Valley.

From Hebron to Port Maitland the landscape is dominated by dairy farms. Along the coast, Sandy Beach Provincial Park is located near the Port Maitland breakwater. A short way up the coast is Bartlett's Beach near Salmon River.

After Salmon River the names of villages and residents take on a decidedly French character. Here Route 1 becomes the province's longest main street with 14 Acadian villages strung out along St. Mary's Bay. This area was settled by Acadians returning to Nova Scotia from places as far away as Louisiana in the years following their expulsion in 1755. Proudly displayed is the tri-colored Acadian flag, with its gold guiding star, the Stella Maris, which led them back to Nova Scotia.

The provincial picnic park at Mavillette is situated on a lovely expanse of white sand and salt marsh rich with bird life. Travelling to Meteghan, note the properties laid out in narrow fishlots running back from the shore front, much like the St. Lawrence's seigneuries.

Meteghan and Meteghan River, whose names are derived from the Micmac word for "blue stone", harbour much of the French Shore's fleet of scallop draggers, trawlers and herring seiners. Settled in the 1770's and 80's by Acadians, a vignette of early Acadian life can be experienced at La Vielle Maison Museum.

Comeauville is the centre of a thriving pâté à la râpure, or rappie pie bakery. This distinctive Acadian dish is made from grated potatoes from which all moisture has been squeezed, baked with chicken, beef, clams or, occasionally, rabbit.

Church Point is the site of Nova Scotia's only bilingual college, Université Sainte-Anne. The campus is dominated by St. Mary's Church, the tallest and largest wooden church in North America.

Along the coast you will pass through Grosses Coques, meaning "large clams", famed for the huge clams dug along the nearby beach and Belliveau's Cove. At St. Bernard a gothic-style granite church dominates the village. Construction of this church took 32 years, beginning in 1910, with all the labour and materials supplied by the local people.

Weymouth was settled by Loyalists in 1783 as a river port for ship building and the shipment of lumber. From here to Digby forestry is the main industry. Many of the villages along this coast

THE FAMOUS DIGBY SCALLOP FLEET - ONE OF THE LARGEST IN THE WORLD *The boats of the famous Digby Scallop Fleet are specially designed for work in the scallop beds. They must be well built to operate in the Atlantic Ocean since their daily travel exposes them to some very rough weather. Delicious Digby scallops are enjoyed all over the world.*

were busy seaports with shipyards and large wharves during the 18th and 19th centuries.

Situated on the Annapolis Basin and sheltered by the passage through Digby Gut is the town of Digby. With a fine provincially-owned resort, the Pines, the world-famous Digby scallop fishing fleet and fish processing plants, Digby is the terminal for car-ferry traffic to Saint John, New Brunswick. Note the traditional fish weirs along the coast. These weirs form huge corrals for netting herring during the summer months when the fish are plentiful. When smoked, these herring are known as "Digby chicks". A side-trip along Route 217 down Digby Neck will take you through a beautiful, little-travelled area of the province. From the fishing ports that dot the peninsula and its attendant islands, boats may be chartered in order to watch the whales which yearly visit the Bay of Fundy to feed on schools of herring.

Smiths Cove, near the Bear River bridges is a popular family resort area with swimming, tennis, sailing and beaches. Ten minutes inland is Bear River, the "Switzerland of Nova Scotia." From here you can cross back to Deep Brook or farther along the Minas Basin to Clementsport and Upper Clements. Upper Clements Park is a family-oriented theme park with gardens, Victorian and Acadian pavilions, arts and crafts and amusement rides.

Annapolis Royal was founded in 1604 by the French and named Port-Royal. The successful preservation of centuries-old buildings like the Adams-Ritchie House (1712) and the integration of an almost four century old history with modern life can be experienced in a walking tour of the town. The Annapolis Royal Historical

EARLY MORNING FOG, WEST-PORT, BRIAR ISLAND, AT THE END OF DIGBY NECK *Digby Neck is a long narrow strip of land between the Bay of Fundy and St. Mary's Bay, which is noted for its beautiful scenery and interesting geological features. Beginning at the top of Digby Neck you pass through Rossway, Centerville, Sandy Cove, Little River, Tiddville and arrive at East Ferry. Here you take the car ferry to Tiverton, then continue through Central Grove to Freeport where you board another car ferry to Westport on Briar Island. Here you will find some striking columnar masses, as well as a large concentration of birds. Whales frequent the waters in summer.*

Gardens cover 10 acres of land with theme gardens featuring roses, Acadian plantings, a maze and Governor's Garden intertwined with almost a mile of pathways.

Fort Anne is Canada's oldest National Historic Park and a well-preserved example of Vauban earthwork fortifications. The present structure, completed in 1710 by the British, is the fourth fort to occupy this ground.

Across the Annapolis River is Granville Ferry, the first of many Valley towns settled by New England Planters in 1759. A short drive toward the Bay of Fundy will take you to the Port Royal Habitation, site of the earliest European settlement north of Florida. The present reconstruction was finished in 1940 from Champlain's original sketches and uses the joinery and hardware of early 17th century France. The original trading post was the home of North America's first social club, The Order of Good Cheer. Grand Micmac Chief Membertou, an early Catholic convert was a "member, too." In 1613 the Habitation was plundered and destroyed by a raiding party from Virginia.

Route 1 on the north side of the Annapolis River and Route 201 on the south meander through the Annapolis Valley towns of Bridgetown, Paradise, Lawrencetown and Middleton. Originally the Valley was settled by the French in the 1650's. The British governor carried out an expulsion in 1755 after the Acadians refused to sign a written oath of allegiance which they felt could someday pit them against their mother country. The rich farmlands expropriated by the British were then granted to New England Planters who settled over the next two decades. Many of their descendants still work these farms growing fruit, vegetables, grain and livestock. Farmers' markets are a common roadside treat, and many farms are "U-pick" operations where the whole family can harvest berries, fruit and vegetables in season.

Greenwood is the location of Canada's largest anti-submarine base as well as headquarters for Search and Rescue operations.

The rich farmlands of the Annapolis Valley are sheltered by two ranges of glacial hills, the North and South Mountains. Crossing the North will take you to the Bay of Fundy; the South reveals small pocket valleys such as Nictaux and Gaspereau.

Kentville is the largest town in the Valley, with a variety of visitor services, shops, walking trails and a park. The Kentville Agricultural Research Station hosts guided tours with an on-site museum and modern research facilities.

Turn north at Greenwich onto Route 358. This road will take you across the dyke-lands started in the 17th century by the Acadians in a successful effort to drain, sweeten and farm the native salt marshes along the Cornwallis River. The tides raise and lower the

THE LARGEST WOODEN CHURCH IN NORTH AMERICA *Part of the campus of Université Ste. Anne, St. Mary's Church is the tallest and largest wooden church in North America. The spire is 185 ft. tall with 40 tons of rock used as a ballast. Construction of the church was completed in 1905.*

river in Port Williams by more than 20 feet. Prescott House, a provincial museum on Starrs Point, was the 1814 Georgian-style home of horticulturalist Charles Ramage Prescott who introduced the Gravenstein and other varieties of apples to the Valley. Route 358 will take you up North Mountain to the look-off from which a breathtaking view of the valley can be had. The road continues to Scotts Bay on Cape Blomidon with its towering cliffs, rocky beach and treasures of amethyst and agates.

Wolfville is home of the 250 acre campus of Acadia University. Founded in 1838 by the Baptists, the original campus was built from timber felled on-site. Today it is a major co-educational, non-denominational university.

Grand Pré, "the great meadow" is situated on extensive dyke-lands and was one of the earliest French settlements in the province. It provided the setting for Longfellow's poem Evangeline chronicling the expulsion of the Acadians in 1755. The site of the Acadian church of Saint-Charles, reconstructed in 1922, sits amidst a grove of weeping willows in quiet pastureland and is now a National Historic Park. In Grand Pré you will also find vineyards and an estate winery.

Where the St. Croix joins the Avon River, midway between the equator and North Pole, there sits the town of Windsor, gateway to the Annapolis Valley. Windsor was founded by the French in 1703, although a 1685 census shows a few families already living there. The British erected Fort Edward in 1750 and the town grew up around this site. Haliburton House, home of Judge Thomas Chandler Haliburton, creator of the fictional Yankee trader "Sam Slick"

CHURCH OF ST. CHARLES AND THE STATUE OF EVANGELINE
The church is a replica of the original Acadian church and contains one of the finest collections of Acadian relics existing today. It was from this church, on September 10, 1755, that the Acadians were taken and sent to New England, Louisiana, the West Indies, and other places. Following the peace of 1763 many returned to Nova Scotia where their descendants live today. Grand Pré means "the great meadow" and refers to the extensively dyked lands in this area. Remains of these dykes may still be seen today.

NORTH MOUNTAIN LOOK-OFF, CANNING   *Located on the Habitant River, Canning is in the fertile Annapolis Valley. One of its early names was Apple Tree Landing. The name Canning was adopted in 1830 in honour of British Prime Minister George Canning.*

THESE TWO PICTURES OF LOW AND HIGH TIDES WERE TAKEN SIX HOURS APART.

is a provincially-operated museum. It was Slick who coined such phrases as "raining cats and dogs" and "truth is stranger than fiction".

At Newport Corner, Route 215 will take you north through Brooklyn toward the Minas Basin. Follow the eastern bank of the Avon through Summerville to Kempt Shore, Cheverie and Cambridge where side roads grant access to the beaches. A side-trip from Noel, so named by the original Acadian settlers, takes you to Burncoat Head, the point at which the highest tides in the world have been scientifically recorded. At Noel the remains of Acadian dyke-lands can still be seen. The forests along Noel Shore once supported a thriving shipbuilding industry. Along this shore you can clearly see the cliffs of Colchester and Cumberland Counties along the Minas Basin's northern shore.

The village of Maitland is situated at the mouth of the Shubenacadie River. Lawrence House, a provincial museum and National Historic Site, commemorates the W. D. Lawrence, the largest wooden ship ever built in Canada. The tidal bore can be viewed from the Maitland Picnic Look-Off. The Shubenacadie River provides nesting and hunting grounds for bald eagles. Route 14 takes you back through the winding Rawdon Hills to Brooklyn.

Mount Uniacke was named after the summer home of Richard John Uniacke who was attorney general of Nova Scotia in 1797. His magnificent 5000 acre colonial estate was completed in 1830 and is now a provincial museum. It is considered to be one of Canada's finest examples of colonial architecture and is filled with a large collection of authentic furnishings.

# THE GLOOSCAP & SUNRISE TRAILS

CENTRAL AND NORTHERN NOVA SCOTIA

TIDAL BORE, TRURO - ONE OF THE GREAT NATURAL WONDERS OF THE WORLD *This is a natural phenomenon which is seen in only a few parts of the world. The Bay of Fundy has the highest tides in the world and because of the "funneling" shape of the river this advancing tide becomes a wave called "Tidal Bore".*

Follow Route 2 from Halifax through Bedford to Waverly. An 1861 Goldrush saw the founding of this village on the banks of the old Shubenacadie Canal System. The road winds through forest and lake-lands from Fall River to Laurie Park on Grand Lake. In neighbouring Oakfield is Oakfield Provincial Park with a small lakeside beach.

Near the Halifax International Airport, Route 2 crosses Highway 102 and shadows it through the villages of Enfield, Elmsdale and Lantz. From Lantz, Route 277 turns inland to Gays River.

Continuing on Route 2 will take you through the market town of Shubenacadie. When the Europeans arrived in Nova Scotia, Shubenacadie was the largest Micmac Indian village in Acadia. Today it is still the main centre of native government. Route 224 to the east will take you through Gays River into the Musquodoboit Valley.

Shubenacadie Provincial Wildlife Park is a 50-acre wildlife park set in a natural woodland. It features many species of animals native to the province.

North on Route 2 are the dairy farms surrounding Brookfield. Here, Route 289 through the Stewiacke Valley intersects Highway 2. Another 15 minutes will take you into Truro at the head of the Minas Basin and Cobequid Bay.

The "Hub of Nova Scotia", Truro, has been a major railroad centre since 1858. With shopping, manufacturing and a variety of visitor services, Truro is the regional centre for Central Nova Scotia. The Nova Scotia Agricultural College and the Nova Scotia Teachers College both make their homes here. Victoria Park, a 1,000-acre forest in the centre of town, features streams, nature trails, a swimming pool, playground and picnic park. Exiting the town to the north is the Salmon River, one of the best places to view the "tidal bore", a wall of water rushing up the shallow river mouth when the tide turns.

Continue on Route 2 through Onslow and Masstown. A few minutes inland from Masstown is Debert, one of the oldest communities in what is now Canada. Debert was a paleo-Indian settlement where artifacts dating back 10,000 years have been found.

At Glenholme, Highway 104 runs inland through the popular ski area of the Wentworth Valley to the small agricultural town of Oxford, "Canada's Blueberry Capital".

From Masstown, Route 2 follows the northern shore of the Minas Basin. As you travel west along the coast, you will see the cliffs across the Basin rising to culminate at Blomidon and Cape Split. At Bass River is the Dominion Chair Company which has been in

HISTORIC FIVE ISLANDS, LO-CATED JUST OUTSIDE TRURO ON THE ROAD TO PARRSBORO *According to Indian legend, these are great pieces of earth which their god, Glooscap threw in anger at the beaver. The islands are called (from east to west) Moose, Diamond, Long, Egg and Pinnacle, and stand so close together that at one time they must have formed one piece of land. To the east is the lonely rock known as "The Old Wife". Moose Island is believed to be the hiding place of much pirate treasure.*

operation since 1860 and has been levelled by fires three times. Where the Economy River enters the Basin is Economy Point where 50 foot tides are common.

Five Islands Provincial Park features camping, hiking and a beach. Micmac legend has it that Glooscap, the mythical warrior who made his home across the Minas at Blomidon, created the five islands when he threw handfuls of sod at Beaver who mocked his powers. The islands are named Diamond, Long, Egg, Pinnacle and Moose. Moose Island is reputed to have buried pirate treasure.

The cliffs of Parrsboro are a haven for rockhounds seeking amethyst and agate, as well as a treasure trove for fossil hunters. The largest collection of fossilized bones ever unearthed in Canada was found near here. Here Route 2 turns northeast toward Springhill.

Route 209 continues along the Minas Basin. The communities of Advocate Harbour and Apple River are perched on Cape Chignecto, which was first mapped by Samuel de Champlain in 1607. The rock formations "Three Sisters", the legendary three sisters of Glooscap who were turned to stone, lie off this treacherous coast.

Springhill gets its name from the spring-fed brooks that form the headwaters of the Maccan River. Large scale coal-mining began here in 1872, and since then three major disasters have taken almost 250 miners' lives. The Springhill Miners' museum features exhibits and underground tours. From here Route 2 swings northward to Amherst.

Amherst, the regional centre of Cumberland County, is built on rising ground at the southern edge of the Tantramar Marsh. As first an Acadian settlement and then an English town, Amherst has been settled since 1672.

Route 6 leads eastward from Amherst following the southern edge of the world's largest marsh until it reaches the Northumberland Strait. It is along the Northumberland shore that you will find beaches with the warmest water in the province. The seasonal lobster fishery operates from late spring until early autumn when the Strait is ice-free.

Here, you can either continue along Route 6, or follow the shore road to Wallace. You will find roadside beaches and picnic parks along the length of the shore road, and at the head of Wallace Bay is a game sanctuary for migratory birds. Route 6 continues across Malagash Point. The only evidence of the salt-mining industry that thrived from 1918 to 1956, when it moved up the shore near Pugwash, is a miner's

JACOBS LADDER, 177 STEPS TO A PANORAMIC VIEW OF TRURO
Victoria Park is a magnificent natural park and was donated to the town of Truro for the pleasure and enjoyment of the people by W.R. Ross. Mr. Ross, who built the "ladder", likened the climb to Jacob ascending into the heavens, hence the name. There are 177 steps and a climb of 180 feet. Other features of Victoria Park include two waterfalls, winding footpaths and a swimming pool all in a picturesque setting.

CAPE SPLIT *Accessible by walking trail only. Cape Split is the perfect vantage point for watching the world's highest tides rise and fall along the Bay of Fundy. Tides here have measured a rise and fall of over 50 feet. Indian legend has it that the MicMac god Glooscap split the rock with his axe. Photo by Kevin Smith.*

cemetery. Included in the farms you will find along this route is the province's second estate vineyard and winery.

Tatamagouche, meaning "meeting place of the waters" is situated at the mouths of the French and Waugh rivers. From here Route 311 will take you across the isthmus to Truro. At Balmoral Mills is the Balmoral Grist Mill, established in 1874 and now a museum.

Route 6 continues from Tatamagouche to the Pictou rotary, passing through dairy farms and lobster fishing villages. Along this stretch of coastline there are numerous tan-coloured sand beaches.

At the Pictou Rotary Highway 106 turns north to the village of Caribou and the summer car-ferries to Prince Edward Island. Nesting cormorants, and the large kraft paper mill in Abercrombie can be seen from the causeway crossing Pictou Harbour.

Pictou was settled in 1773 by the first Scottish Highlanders to reach the province. Pictou has a wonderful collection of early 19th century wooden and stone heritage houses. The 1904 Canadian National Railway station now houses the Northumberland Fisheries Museum. McCulloch House Museum is the 1806 home of Thomas McCulloch who founded Pictou Academy and became Dalhousie College's first president.

Trenton is an industrial town with a large steel forging plant, rail car works and other heavy industry. New Glasgow is the main commercial and service centre for Pictou County. Its situation between the coal mines of Stellarton and steel plant at Trenton made

it the province's industrial giant at the turn of the last century. From
the remains of an old stone pump-house on the Foord coal seam, the
Nova Scotia Museum of Industry and Transportation has been constructed. At the Pictou County Historical Museum you can see
Canada's oldest steam locomotive, the "Samson". The "Samson"
hauled coal cars from the mines to the piers on Canada's oldest steel
railway.

Coal mines have been in operation since the discovery of
the Foord coal seam in Stellarton in 1798. Nearby Westville was
named for the new coal-mining operations established here in the
1860's which are west of earlier Pictou County Mines.

Route 289 runs from Westville to Brookfield across the
interior of the province. The highway twists through small valleys
and over forested hills. Much of the timber for the paper mill in
Abercrombie is harvested in this part of Pictou and Colchester Counties.
In Eastville you emerge from the forests into the Stewiacke Valley.
Upper and Middle Stewiacke are quiet farming settlements along the
elm-shaded river.

From Upper Stewiacke you can cross the range of hills
separating the Stewiacke and Musquodoboit River Valleys and follow
Route 224 through more forest to Sheet Harbour or through the dairy
farms down the Musquodoboit River to Stewiacke. An alternative is
Route 357 which runs from Middle Musquodoboit to Musquodoboit
Harbour on the Eastern Shore.

A PIPER'S WELCOME *One of the most colourful entrances to any province, these sunken gardens and the skirl of the bagpipes provide a memorable welcome to Nova Scotia.*

LOBSTER BOATS AT REST, TONEY RIVER, PICTOU COUNTY *This serene, rural area on the Northumberland Shore offers the photographer a gem for his hobby. The river and settlement are said to have been named after a Captain Toney, a Frenchman, and the Micmac name was "Booktowoogen", the place for fire, i.e. flint. Since fishing and farming are the basic industries here, visitors enjoy sightseeing and souvenir hunting.*

THE MARINE DRIVE

EASTERN SHORE AND THE CABOT STRAIT

Leave Dartmouth via Portland Street. At Cole Harbour, now a suburban area, Portland Street becomes Route 207. If you take the last right hand turn leaving Cole Harbour, the road will take you out to the Cole Harbour Marsh and dyke-lands. Rainbow Haven Provincial Beach is located at the seaward edge of this marsh. A short distance from this junction, Route 208 leads inland to Preston, the oldest Black community in Canada, settled by the Jamaican Maroons in 1784.

Continue on Route 207 through Lawrencetown to the Provincial Beach. Beware the first beach you come to, as the undertow at the mouth of the river is extremely hazardous. The second beach is fully supervised by lifeguards. Route 207 continues through the Acadian-settled villages of Grand Desert and West Chezzetcook before joining Highway 7.

Route 357 from the Musquodoboit Valley intersects Route 7 at Musquodoboit Harbour, the main service centre at this end of the Eastern Shore. Follow the coastal road out to Martinique Beach. This

FROM YARMOUTH TO CAPE BRETON, TRAVELLERS ARE DELIGHTED BY THIS ROADSIDE COLOUR *While travelling throughout many parts of Nova Scotia, visitors will delight in scenes like this. Great masses of blue-violet lupines, occasionally mixed with pink or white, covering acreas of hills, and stretching along roadside banks. Two naturalized species, native from California to Alaska, here grow together and freely intercross. Heavier areas of concentrations are found in Yarmouth County, the South Shore, Eastern Shore and Truro.*

three mile stretch of supervised white sand is the longest beach in Nova Scotia. At Clam Harbour, along the coast is another hard white-sand beach.

As you drive along the coast into Ship Harbour you will see thousands of white buoys. Ship Harbour is the site of North America's largest cultivated mussel farm. Taylor's Head Provincial Park sits at the tip of Taylor's Head outside Spry Harbour. The white sand beach overlooks two bays.

Sheet Harbour was founded in 1784 by refugees from the American Revolution. Originally a lumbering centre, Sheet Harbour is now a regional service centre. From here you can follow the East River Sheet Harbour inland to Liscomb Game Sanctuary covering 200 square miles of nature preserve.

Continue along the twisted, barren coast through fishing villages such as Spanish Bay, where aquaculture operations raise oysters, trout and salmon, to Sherbrooke. Sherbrooke sits on the banks of the St. Mary's river at the site where the French trader La Giraudière built his 1655 trading post. Today, Sherbrooke village is a major historical restoration project. Some 30 buildings and homes have been restored and form a living museum of the period from 1860 to 1880.

Route 7 turns inland at Sherbrooke to follow the St. Mary's River to its headwaters and then on to Antigonish.

Approximately five minutes inland from Sherbrooke, Route 211 cuts back toward the coast, following it through Port Bickerton to

SHERBROOKE VILLAGE   Sherbrooke was originally a fur-trading post built in 1655. Farming, lumbering, fishing and shipbuilding were carried on in this community, and in 1861 gold mining brought 20 years of prosperity. Now, much of Sherbrooke has been restored as it was in the 1860-80 period. Photo courtesy Nova Scotia Museum.

the ferry across the Country Harbour. Continuing along the coast on Route 316 you will pass several beaches including the Provincial Picnic Park at Tor Bay.

A few miles east of the junction of Route 316 and Route 16 sits the town of Canso. Canso is the most easterly point on continental North America. With the large harbour sheltered by Grassy Island, Canso was an established French fishing station in the 1500's. The British built a fort on Grassy Island in 1720 which is today a National Historic Site.

Canso derives its name from the Micmac for "opposite the lofty cliffs." Drive westward along the shore of Chedabucto Bay for a phenomenal view of these cliffs.

Guysborough is the site of another 17th century French fishing station. English pioneers arrived in the 1760's and were later augmented by United Empire Loyalists. The restored Courthouse is the local museum.

From Guysborough you can follow Route 16 across country to Monastery where it meets Route 4, or take Route 344 along the northern shore of Chedabucto Bay and the Canso Strait to Mulgrave. The industrial base of Mulgrave and Port Hawkesbury have benefitted from an ice-free harbour formed with the construction of the nearby Canso Causeway to Cape Breton. The causeway is the deepest in the world.

West on Route 4 will take you through the parishes of Havre Boucher, Monastery and Tracadie. At Tracadie and nearby

HAVING BEEN CLEANED, SPLIT AND SALTED, THESE FISH LAY DRYING IN THE SUN *Typical fishing scene around Nova Scotia's coast. The fish are cleaned, salted and placed on "fish flakes" to dry in the sun. Fresh, frozen or salted, Nova Scotia's fish travels to all parts of the globe.*

Pomquet, settled by Acadian immigrants from St. Milo in 1761, you will find beaches bathed by the warm waters of the Northumberland Strait.

St. Francis Xavier University in the town of Antigonish has won international recognition for its part in the co-operative and credit union movement. The Coady Institute offers a co-op program training students from some 80 countries in community development. Antigonish is the regional centre for the county and home of the Antigonish Highland Games which have been held continuously since 1861.

From Antigonish, Route 4 travels across country through the sheltered vales of Marshy Hope and Barney's River to New Glasgow. Alternatively, Route 337 hugs the cliffs of Cape George, offering spectacular views of the Northumberland Strait. Along this coast and on Route 245 you will find several sheltered, deserted beaches.

Along the coast around Merigomish Harbour are more popular beaches, including the fully-supervised Melmerby Provincial Beach.

ARISAIG - ON THE BEAUTIFUL SUNRISE TRAIL *Located northwest of Antigonish on the Northumberland Strait, Arisaig takes its name from a district in Western Scotland. Arisaig features a beautiful beach and scenery sure to please any visitor.*

SCHOONER RACE IN THE BLUE ATLANTIC WATERS
What a beautiful sight as these schooners race across the blue Atlantic waters under full sail! Nova Scotia is famous for its shipbuilding, which includes a replica of the Bounty, and both Bluenose I and II.

ONE OF THE MANY RESTORED BUILDINGS, SHERBROOKE VILLAGE
In the period 1860-1880, Sherbrooke was a major centre. Much of Sherbrooke has been restored including the general store, blacksmith shop, emporium, post office, woodworking shop and tea room.

"CIAD MILE FAILTE"
A Hundred
Thousand
Welcomes

PRESQU'ILE ON THE CABOT TRAIL
This is just one of the many scenic views you will find along the Cabot Trail. The Cabot Trail consists of a circular highway 184 miles long, passing through some of the world's most spectacular scenery.

THE TRAILS OF CAPE BRETON

INCLUDING HISTORIC LOUISBOURG

"Ciad mile failte" is Gaelic for a hundred thousand welcomes. Once you've crossed the Canso Causeway to Cape Breton Island, the spectacular beauty of this diverse island and distinctive culture of its people will welcome you to this province within a province.

Cape Breton is almost 4,000 square miles in size, with highlands in the north, rolling hills and river valleys in the south and a large inland sea, Bras d'Or Lake, in the middle.

At the Port Hastings rotary three choices for exploration await you. Route 19 travels the northwestern shore of the Island, joining with the Cabot Trail at Margaree Forks. Highway 105 cuts across country to Whycocomagh from which it follows the northern shore of the Bras d'Or. Routes 104 and 4 follow the southeastern coast of the island to St. Peters and then along the south coast of Bras d'Or and down the Sydney River to Sydney.

Route 19 along the eastern shoreline of Inverness County will take you past no less than 17 beaches. Port Hood Island was the quarry for much of the stone used to construct the Fortress of

PANORAMIC VIEW OF THE ALEXANDER GRAHAM BELL MUSEUM, BADDECK *Officially opened in 1956, this striking building houses a fascinating display relating to the various fields of science. Here you will find exhibits of the early telephones Bell invented, as well as early flying models. It was here in Baddeck, Nova Scotia, that the first British Empire Aeroplane flight took place in 1909. Photo by Ray Martheleur.*

Louisbourg. Mabou is a beautiful valley tucked between rolling hills, and centre of a thriving Scottish culture. Gaelic is taught as a second language in the local school. Follow Route 252 to Whycocomagh or continue through Glenville and Strathlorne to Inverness. Inverness features a Miners' Museum and supervised beach. Route 19 joins the Cabot Trail at Margaree Forks. Follow the Margaree River through magnificent valley scenery to Baddeck.

The most direct route to Baddeck from the Canso Causeway is Highway 105 which stretches across Inverness County to Whycocomagh on the western side of Bras d'Or Lake. Whycocomagh means "head of the waters" in Micmac, and today is a Micmac reserve and community descended from Highland Scots.

East of Whycocomagh a car ferry across Little Narrows and another between Iona and Grand Narrows will take you along Route 223 and St. Andrews Channel to Sydney. If you take this route you'll want binoculars to observe the bald eagles which nest along the shores of Bras d'Or.

Highway 105 continues along the northern shore of Bras d'Or to Baddeck. Baddeck is the largest community on Bras d'Or Lake and features several resorts and a supervised beach.

The Alexander Graham Bell National Park, at the eastern end of town sits across the bay from Beinn Breagh, where Bell spent the last 37 years of his life. On display at the exhibit centre are artifacts and photographs telling the life story of this inventor, teacher and humanitarian.

Lunenburg by day and night

Ross Farm has been restored as a working farm museum

Farther along Highway 105, in Englishtown, is the gravesite of Angus McAskill (1825-1863), the "Cape Breton Giant". At 7'9" tall, McAskill is the tallest non-pathological giant on record.

From Englishtown, a sideroad leads to a car ferry across St. Ann's Bay to the Cabot Trail. The communities clustered around St. Ann's Bay form the heart of the Cape Breton Scottish Highlands. The Gaelic College is the only one of its kind in North America. During the summer months it offers courses in all the Highlands' arts and crafts including, of course, bagpipes and features a Great Hall of the Clans.

The Cabot Trail continues up the northeast coast of Cape Breton climbing the mist-shrouded peaks of Cape Smokey. On the other side is Ingonish, the administrative headquarters of Cape Breton Highlands National Park. Ingonish Beach and North Bay feature two

THE BRAS D'OR LAKES, A YACHT-MAN'S PARADISE *On February 23, 1909 the tranquility of the Bras d'Or Lakes was disrupted by the roar of the engines of the "Silver Dart". She was a project of Alexander Graham Bell and his associates, also known as the Aerial Experiment Association, and on that day made the first airplane flight within the British Empire.*

MONUMENT TO GIANT McASKILL *In loving memory of Angus McAskill, the Nova Scotian Giant, who died at his home in St. Ann's, August 6, 1863. Age 38 years, height 7 ft. 9 in., girth 80 in., weight 425 lbs.*

supervised beaches. The provincially-owned Keltic Resort is located in Middle Head. The Portuguese had summer fishing camps here as early as 1521. Travel along the Atlantic Coast past lookoffs, trails, rocky headlands and the fishing community of Neil Harbour to Dingwall. Dingwall has sand beaches and twin lighthouses. At Cape North a detour off the trail will take you to Bay St. Lawrence and Cabot's Landing, believed to be the place visited by John and Sebastian Cabot in 1497. From here the trail turns westward and down the slopes of Cape Smokey through the maples of the Grand Anse Valley to Pleasant Bay. From Pleasant Bay the Trail climbs MacKenzie Mountain through a series of switchbacks and sweeps through broad barrens and along the spectacular rocky coastal cliffs. At Cheticamp you exit the National Park.

Acadians expelled from mainland Nova Scotia settled on Cheticamp Island in 1755. Today the island features a lovely beach and picturesque lighthouse. The Acadians spread out along this coast, founding such communities as Petit Etang, Grand Etang, St. Joseph du Moine and Belle Cote. From Margaree Forks, the Cabot Trail continues through the Margaree Valley to Route 105 in Baddeck.

East of Englishtown, Highway 105 climbs and then steeply descends Kelly's Mountain. The switchbacks leading down to Seal Island Bridge afford a marvellous view of Great Bras d'Or, connecting the lake with the Atlantic. The scenic shore route through Big Bras d'Or takes you along the rugged coastline. Offshore are Bird Islands, nesting grounds for cormorants, puffins, petrels, razorbills and terns.

SPECTACULAR AUTUMN COLOUR IN THE CAPE BRETON HIGHLANDS *Fiery red, deep orange and brilliant rust are some of the spectacular colours that are found along the Cabot Trail in the autumn. Combined with the rolling hills, this colourful array of leaves in autumn draws visitors from near and far to enjoy this spectacle. The Cabot Trail is 184 miles of one of the most scenic drives in North America. Photo by Ray Martheleur.*

Coal mining in Sydney Mines began in 1766. The mines stretch for miles out under the sea. At North Sydney ferries sail to Newfoundland.

The third highway from the Canso Causeway to Sydney is Route 4. Port Hawkesbury, home of the Nova Scotia Nautical Institute, is an industrial town reliant upon shipping in the Canso Strait. Following the southern coast of Cape Breton will take you past Isle Madame to St. Peters. It takes about an hour to drive around Isle Madame which was settled by Acadians in the early mid-1700's. The island features a museum at Arichat, the original site of St. Francis Xavier College, a manned lighthouse at Cap Rouge, beaches and picnic areas.

At St. Peters, Route 4 crosses the St. Peter's Canal. Started in 1854, this single-lock canal connects Bras d'Or Lake with St. Peter's Bay on the Atlantic. Nicolas Denys established a fur trading post at what the Portuguese called San Pedro in 1650. The French established a fort here in 1737. It was captured by the English in 1745, returned to France three years later and recaptured in 1758. The loyalists followed 22 years later. The Nicolas Denys Museum at the canal features exhibits recounting Denys' 19 year career in the New World.

Detour along the coast on Route 247 through L'Ardoise to the long sandy beach at Point Michaud. Route 4 continues along the south coast of Bras d'Or. This road was built in 1788 to facilitate the movement of troops from St. Peters to Sydney. En route to Sydney

THE BREATHTAKING BEAUTY OF CAPE ROUGE, ALONG THE CABOT TRAIL *One of the many beautiful rivers along the Cabot Trail is found here at Cape Rouge. Driving above the sea on this meandering trail, you can enjoy Nova Scotia's scenic beauty all around you.*

A.E.A. SILVER DART *The first aeroplane flight in the British Empire, February 23, 1909. Painting by R.W. Bradford, courtesy National Aviation Museum, Ottawa.*

you will pass the Micmac community of Chapel Island and, if you take a sideroad along the north shore of East Bay, Eskasoni. Eskasoni is the province's largest Micmac reserve.

Clustered around Spanish Bay is Industrial Cape Breton. The economy is based on the heavy industries of coal mining and steel making. Sydney, the third-largest city in the province, was founded by Loyalists in 1785, followed 20 years later by the Scots. Visit Wentworth Park near the city centre, Cossit House (1787) Museum on Charlotte Street and St. Patrick's Church on the waterfront. The University College of Cape Breton is on the eastern outskirts of town, en route to Glace Bay.

With two operating mines, New Waterford is the largest coal-producing town in eastern Canada. Neighbouring Glace Bay is a former mining town and location of a National Historic Site marking Guglielmo Marconi's wireless telegraph station from which the first transatlantic wireless message to Europe was broadcast on December 15, 1902.

Take Route 22 from Sydney which crosses the fabled Mira River on its way to Louisbourg. The town of Louisbourg is surrounded by the nation's largest National Historic Park. The ambitious restoration of the French Fortress of Louisbourg, laid to waste by the British two years after its capture in 1758, has now completed one quarter of the original town and many of its stone fortifications.

In 1713, Nova Scotia, with the exception of Cape Breton, was ceded by treaty to the English. But the French soon made the

most of Cape Breton's strategic location at the mouth of the Gulf of St. Lawrence. Over a period of 24 years, they constructed a massive stone fortress on the harbour at Louisbourg. As well as the fortress, harbour batteries and lighthouse, a town covering 50 acres and sheltered by a two-mile long earthenworks and masonry wall was built to provide the commercial, military and government centre for the colony.

Although massive in size, its actual fortifications were weak, and in 1745 a band of New England volunteers successfully captured Louisbourg. This feat did not rate highly on the scale of world events and in 1748 the British handed the fortress back to France. But French rule in Cape Breton was to last only ten more years. In 1758, the British, this time under the command of General James Wolfe, once again captured Louisbourg. Two years later, British Prime Minister William Pitt ordered its total destruction.

During the summer months costumed "inhabitants" act as your guides through some 40 restored buildings including shops, restaurants and exhibits.

THE CABOT TRAIL IS 184 MILES OF BREATHTAKING SCENERY *The Cabot Trail is one of the most beautiful drives on the continent. This unusual view of a section of the Cabot Trail is found on the north shore between Presqu'ile and Cape Rouge. Here the hills roll gracefully down to the sea offering visitors a spectacular drive along the coast, before climbing to the tops of the mountains, some as high as 1,750 feet above sea level. The Cabot Trail is named after John and Sebastian Cabot, who discovered Cape North, Cape Breton, in 1497.*

PANORAMIC VIEW OF LOUISBOURG
Photo courtesy Parks Canada.

PORTE DAUPHINE - ENTRANCE GATE TO LOUISBOURG   *This faithful recreation of the Fortress of Louisbourg, built originally from 1720-1744, stands as a monument to the historic struggles of early Canada. A visit to Louisbourg will be a treasured memory for young and old alike.*

FOOD PREPARATION AT LOUISBOURG *The town covered more than 50 acres and was surrounded by a masonry and earth packed wall, almost two miles in length. Louisbourg was captured in 1745, handed back to the French in 1748 and recaptured by the British in 1758. The town was then completely demolished. Its reconstruction is in exacting detail, with furnishings of the period. (The book LOUISBOURG FROM ITS FOUNDATION TO ITS FALL by J.S. McLennan gives the complete history of Louisbourg and a fascinating insight into historic everyday life).*

AERIAL VIEW SHOWING THE EAST TIP OF SABLE ISLAND *Photo courtesy Canadian Coast Guard, Dartmouth.*

SABLE ISLAND

GRAVEYARD OF THE ATLANTIC

One hundred and eighty-five miles east-southeast of Nova Scotia is a geographical feature few Nova Scotians have ever visited. There is no way you can visit Sable Island unless you have the permission of the Department of Transportation which administers this protected island. Today, the few temporary residents on the island operate and maintain the meteorological station, two light-houses and radio beacon.

Sable Island is an open crescent-shaped projection of the outer continental shelf; the only such projection off the east coast of North America. It is just over twenty miles in length and one mile wide at its widest point. The tips of the island extend under the sea making it a navigation hazard stretching for fifty miles. Sable Island consists of two parallel sand-dune ridges separated by a depression which features Lake Wallace, a three and a half mile long fresh-water lake.

In spite of several poorly-planned attempts, Sable Island has never been permanently settled. It has seen temporary occupation by shipwrecked sailors, transported convicts, pirates and wreckers, as well as lighthouse keepers, research and weather personnel.

Sable Island earned its nickname "The Graveyard of the Atlantic" honestly. There have been some 300 shipwrecks recorded since the establishment of the first lifestation in 1801. The first is believed to be one of Sir Humphrey Gilbert's ships which foundered in 1583. In 1598 the Marquis de la Roche deposited forty convict settlers on the island. Five years later the twelve survivors were rescued.

Sable Island forms a natural barrier for sand dredged up by the fierce southerly ocean gales that batter the island. These dunes have been captured by marram grass and low shrubs. Animal life is abundant on the island and includes insects, fresh-water aquatic life from Lake Wallace, harbour and grey seals, terns, sandpipers, gulls and the Ipswich sparrow. The Ipswich sparrow is unique to the island and nests nowhere else.

The most famous animal life on the island are the Sable Island ponies. Actually horses, the "ponies", as they are called, are really quite large, weighing 600 to 800 pounds. While they exhibit a great variety of forms and colours, their most distinguishing features are their long flowing manes and tails. They closely resemble the Spanish barb, as well as the Acadian workhorses which were common to Nova Scotia in the seventeenth, eighteenth and nineteenth centuries. Their numbers vary from one hundred and fifty to four hundred, with the population averaging about two hundred and fifty.

SABLE ISLAND "PONIES" ROAM FREELY *Photo courtesy Canadian Coast Guard, Dartmouth.*

WEST NAVIGATIONAL LIGHT, SABLE ISLAND
Photo courtesy Canadian Coast Guard, Dartmouth.

SABLE ISLAND "PONIES" AMID THE SAND DUNES OF SABLE ISLAND
Photo courtesy Canadian Coast Guard, Dartmouth.

THE CONSTANTLY SHIFTING SANDS OF SABLE ISLAND ALMOST BURIED THIS ABANDONED HOUSE *Photo courtesy Canadian Coast Guard, Dartmouth.*

The romantic notion is that the ponies are survivors of the hundreds of ships who have seen ruin on this barrier's shoals. In all probability they are descendants of horses introduced by Andrew LeMercier of Boston, in the middle of the eighteenth century, along with cattle, hogs and sheep in an unsuccessful attempt to start a farming settlement.

No ponies have been removed from the island since 1947. However, Shubenacadie Wildlife Park, between Halifax and Truro, does feature the pony as part of its exhibit of indigenous wildlife.

ANGUS L. MACDONALD BRIDGE AT NIGHT *linking the "twin-cities" of Halifax and Dartmouth*.

Nova Scotia truly is picture-perfect. Where else can you find such scenic variety? Crashing surf and placid lakes, tiny highland hamlets and bustling cities, ancient rites and modern magic - it's all here.

Although only three hundred and fifty miles from tip to tip, Nova Scotia's coastline stretches for almost five thousand miles. Around every bend, a new treasure awaits the explorer.

But the true riches of Nova Scotia are to be found in its people. "Bluenosers" are open, friendly and willing to share in the culture and good times of their province. Our relaxed pace and willingness to stop and "spin a yarn" can lead you to hidden delights not replicated anywhere else. Nova Scotians have been here for centuries. There's no rush. Spend some time with us.